**FIRE SAFETY**

# Stop, Drop, and Roll

by Lucia Raatma

## Bridgestone Books
an imprint of Capstone Press
Mankato, Minnesota

Bridgestone Books are published by Capstone Press
818 North Willow Street, Mankato, Minnesota 56001
http://www.capstone-press.com

*Library of Congress Cataloging-in-Publication Data*
Raatma, Lucia.
    Stop, drop, and roll/by Lucia Raatma.
    p. cm.—(Fire safety)
    Includes bibliographical references and index.
    Summary: Describes how to react safely if your clothes are on fire, by stopping,
dropping to the ground or floor, and rolling to put out the fire.
    ISBN 0-7368-0197-9
    1. Fires—Safety measures—Juvenile literature. 2. Fire prevention—Juvenile
literature. [1. Fires. 2. Safety.] I. Title. II. Series: Raatma, Lucia. Fire safety.
TH9148.R3323 1999
628.9'22—dc21                                                                    98-48482
                                                                                      CIP
                                                                                      AC

**Editorial Credits**
Rebecca Glaser, editor; Timothy Halldin, cover designer and illustrator;
  Kimberly Danger, photo researcher

**Photo Credits**
David F. Clobes, 4, 6, 8, 12, 14, 16, 18, 20, 20 (inset)
Gregg R. Andersen, cover, 10

**Capstone Press would like to thank George A. Miller, Chief of Fire Code
Enforcement, New Jersey Division of Fire Safety, for reviewing this material.**

# Table of Contents

## Safe Fire

Fire has many uses. People use campfires for cooking and warmth. Candles can look nice and give light. But fire also can be dangerous. Fire can burn you. You should keep a safe distance from fire. You should learn what to do if your clothes catch on fire.

## Heat Sources

Heat sources can start fires. Be careful around stoves, fireplaces, and other heat sources. Matches and lighters also are heat sources. Give any matches and lighters you find to adults.

## When to Stop, Drop, and Roll

Loose or baggy clothes easily can catch fire near an open flame. Your clothes also can catch on fire if they touch other heat sources. Learn what to do if your clothes catch on fire. Stop, drop, and roll to put out the fire.

9

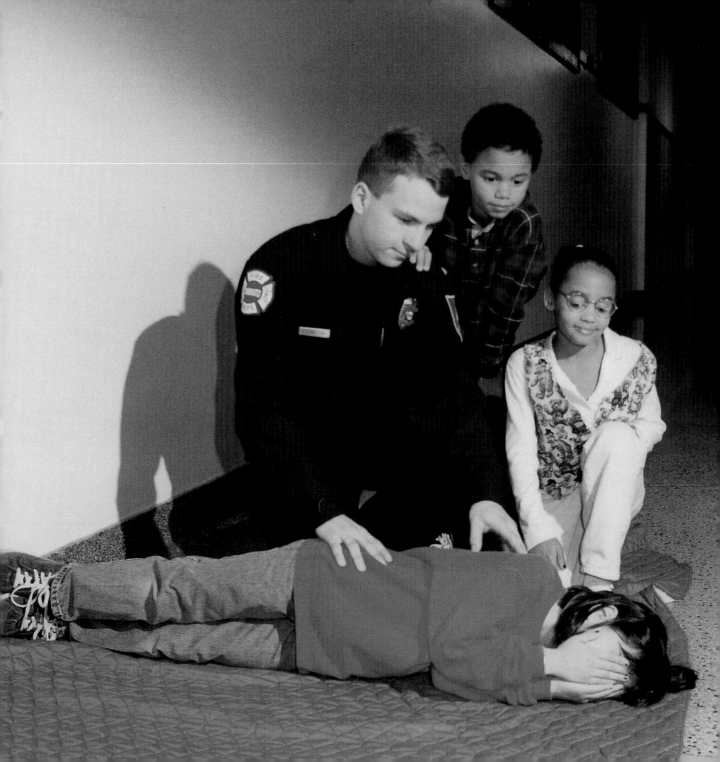

## Oxygen

Fire needs oxygen to burn. Oxygen is a colorless gas in the air. Do not run if your clothes catch on fire. Fire gets more oxygen if you run. You can smother a fire if you stop, drop, and roll.

**smother**

to cover completely; smothering flames will put out a fire.

## Stop

Stop what you are doing if your clothes catch on fire. Do not run. Do not blow on the fire or wave your hands at it. Doing these things will make the flames bigger.

## Drop

After you stop, drop to the ground. Lie flat and cover your face with your hands. Your hands will keep your face from getting burned. Your hands also will help keep you from breathing smoke.

## Roll

After you drop, roll. Rolling should smother the fire. Roll slowly across the ground until your clothes stop burning. Keep your hands over your face until the fire is out.

## Treating Burns

After the fire is out, tell someone to phone 9-1-1. Ask an adult to run cool water over any burns. Emergency workers will help you when they arrive. You may need to go to a hospital if the burn is bad.

**emergency workers**

people who help others in an emergency such as fire

## Fuel

Your clothes can become fuel for a fire. It is important to keep your clothes away from fire. Wear flame-resistant clothes when you can. This kind of clothing does not catch fire easily. Many pajamas are flame-resistant.

21

# Hands On: Stealing Oxygen from a Fire

Fire needs heat, fuel, and oxygen to burn. This experiment shows how taking away oxygen will put out a fire. Remember that oxygen is in the air around us.

## What You Need

Short candle
Empty glass jar with no lid (the jar should be larger than the candle)
An adult to help

## What You Do

1. Have an adult light the candle.
2. Let the flame burn for a few minutes.
3. Cover the candle with the jar.
4. Watch the fire go out. The fire cannot burn because it cannot get enough oxygen from the air inside the jar.

# Words to Know

**flame** (FLAYM)—the moving column of light and heat that a fire gives off

**flame-resistant** (FLAYM-ri-ZISS-tuhnt)—not likely to catch fire

**heat source** (HEET SORSS)—the place where a fire can start

**oxygen** (OK-suh-juhn)—a colorless gas in the air; fire needs oxygen to burn.

**smother** (SMUTH-ur)—to cover completely; smothering flames will put out a fire.

# Read More

**Butler, Daphne.** *What Happens When Fire Burns.* Austin, Texas: Raintree Steck-Vaughn, 1996.

**Loewen, Nancy.** *Fire Safety.* Plymouth, Minn.: Child's World, 1997.

**Raatma, Lucia.** *Safety around Fire.* Safety First! Mankato, Minn.: Bridgestone Books, 1999.

# Internet Sites

**Fire Prevention for Kids**
http://www.prairienet.org/~xx010/FirePreventionForKids1.html

**Sparky's Home Page**
http://www.sparky.org

**U.S. Fire Administration (USFA) Kids Homepage**
http://www.usfa.fema.gov/kids

# Index